ESSENTIAL ELEMENTS

PIANO THEORY

ISBN 978-1-4768-0608-2

HAL•LEONARD®
CORPORATION
7777 W. BLUEMOUND RD. P.O. BOX 13819 MILWAUKEE, WI 53213

In Australia Contact:
Hal Leonard Australia Pty. Ltd.
4 Lentara Court
Cheltenham, Victoria, 3192 Australia
Email: ausadmin@halleonard.com.au

Visit Hal Leonard Online at
www.halleonard.com

To the Student

I wrote these books with you in mind. As a young student I often wondered how completing theory workbooks would make me a better musician. The theory work often seemed separate from the music I was playing. My goal in *Essential Elements Piano Theory* is to provide you with the tools you will need to compose, improvise, play classical and popular music, or to better understand any other musical pursuit you might enjoy. In each "Musical Mastery" section of this book you will experience creative applications of the theory you have learned. The "Ear Training" pages will be completed with your teacher at the lesson. In this series you will begin to learn the building blocks of music, which make it possible for you to have fun at the piano. A practical understanding of theory enables you to see what is possible in music. I wish you all the best on your journey as you learn the language of music!

Sincerely,
Mona Rejino

To the Teacher

I believe that knowledge of theory is most beneficial when a concept is followed directly by a musical application. In *Essential Elements Piano Theory*, learning theory becomes far more than completing worksheets. Students have the opportunity to see why learning a particular concept can help them become a better pianist right away. They can also see how the knowledge of musical patterns and chord progressions will enable them to be creative in their own musical pursuits: composing, arranging, improvising, playing classical and popular music, accompanying, or any other.

A free download of the *Teacher's Answer Key* is available at www.halleonard.com/eeptheory1answer.

Acknowledgements

I would like to thank Hal Leonard Corporation for providing me the opportunity to put these theoretical thoughts down on paper and share them with others. I owe a debt of gratitude to Jennifer Linn, who has helped with this project every step of the way. These books would not have been possible without the support of my family: To my husband, Richard, for his wisdom and amazing ability to solve dilemmas; to my children, Maggie and Adam, for helping me think outside the box.

TABLE OF CONTENTS

Introduction to the Keyboard

The black keys are in groups of  and

1. Circle the groups of **2 BLACK KEYS** on the keyboard below.

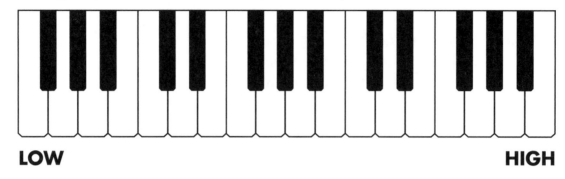

LOW   **HIGH**

2. Circle the groups of **3 BLACK KEYS** on the keyboard below.

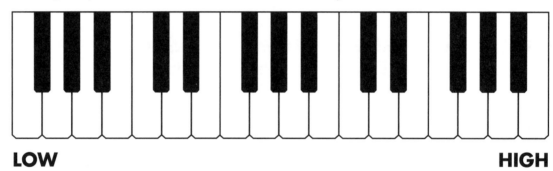

LOW   **HIGH**

Seven letters make up the **MUSIC ALPHABET: A B C D E F G**
These letters are used over and over to name the **WHITE KEYS** on the keyboard.

3. Write the music alphabet.

A _____ _____ _____ _____ _____ _____

4. Write the music alphabet 2 times going up the keyboard.

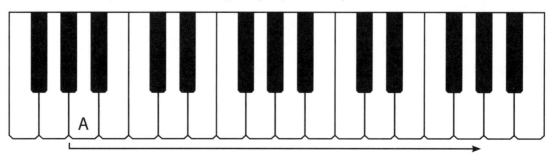

5. Write the music alphabet 2 times going down the keyboard.

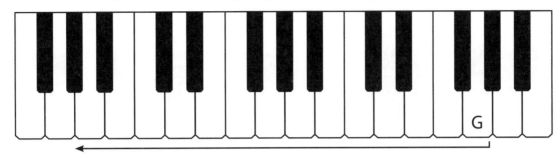

C is to the left of the 2 black key groups.

6. Write the C D E letter names on the white keys below.

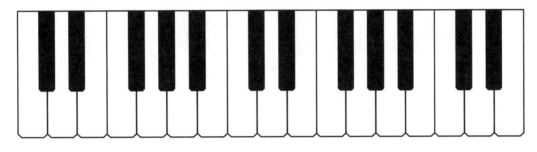

F is to the left of the 3 black key groups.

7. Write the F G A B letter names on the white keys below.

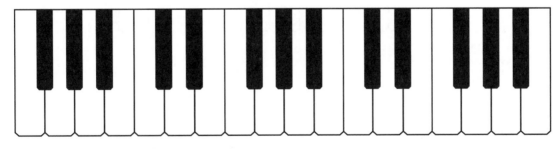

8. Fill in the missing letters from the music alphabet.

A ____ C   D ____ F   G ____ B   C ____ E

____ D ____   ____ G ____   ____ C ____   ____ F

9. Name the shaded keys in the blanks below. Each keyboard spells a word.

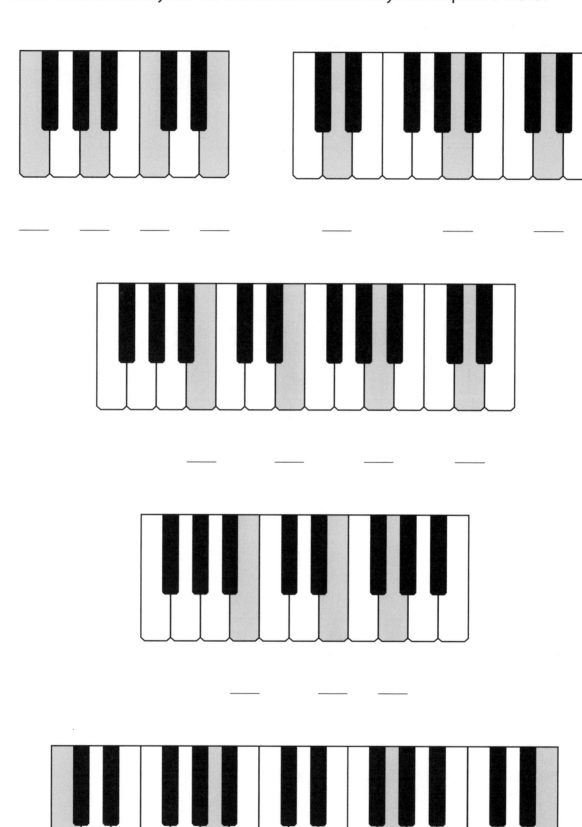

Rhythms

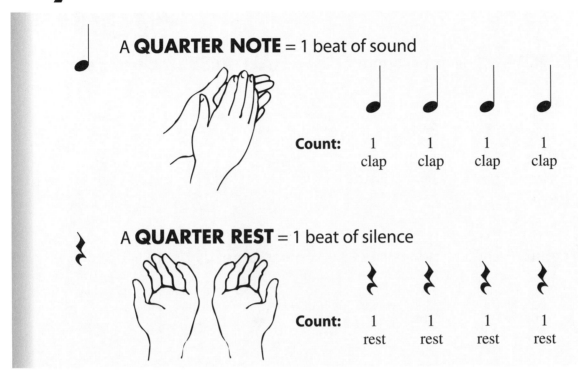

A **QUARTER NOTE** = 1 beat of sound

Count: 1 1 1 1
clap clap clap clap

A **QUARTER REST** = 1 beat of silence

Count: 1 1 1 1
rest rest rest rest

1. Clap and count the notes and rests below, keeping a steady beat.

BAR LINES divide music into **MEASURES**. A **DOUBLE BAR LINE** marks the end of a piece.

2. Trace the bar lines and double bar line below.

3. Fill each measure with 4 beats. Use quarter notes and quarter rests.

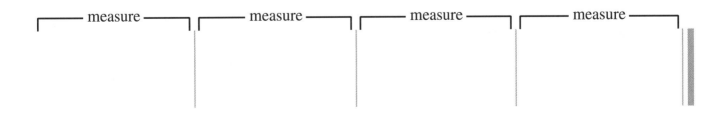

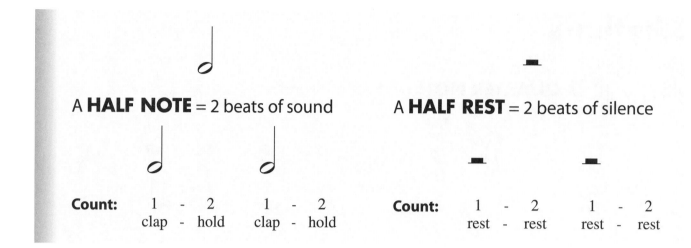

A **HALF NOTE** = 2 beats of sound

Count: 1 - 2   1 - 2
clap - hold   clap - hold

A **HALF REST** = 2 beats of silence

Count: 1 - 2   1 - 2
rest - rest   rest - rest

4. Clap and count the notes and rests below, keeping a steady beat.

5. Trace the bar lines and double bar line below.

6. Fill each measure with 4 beats. Use half notes and half rests.

A **REPEAT SIGN** is formed by placing dots in front of a double bar line. A repeat sign means to play the piece again.

Double Bar Line

Repeat Sign

7. Add a repeat sign at the end of the rhythm below.

8. Clap and count the rhythm two times.

A **WHOLE NOTE** = 4 beats of sound

A **WHOLE REST** = 4 beats of silence

Count: 1 - 2 - 3 - 4
        clap - hold - hold - hold

Count: 1 - 2 - 3 - 4
        rest - rest - rest - rest

9. Clap and count the notes and rests below, keeping a steady beat.

10. Trace the bar lines and double bar line below.

11. Fill each measure with 4 beats. Use whole notes and whole rests.

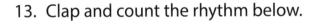

12. Fill each measure below with 4 beats. You may use quarter notes, quarter rests, half notes, half rests, whole notes and whole rests.

13. Clap and count the rhythm below.

Directional Reading

1. Write the **FINGER NUMBERS** on each hand below. Begin with number "1" on the thumbs and end with number "5" on the pinkies.

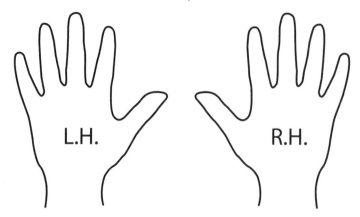

2. Write "L.H." inside each left hand and "R.H." inside each right hand.

STEM DIRECTION: Stems Up = Right Hand

Stems Down = Left Hand

3. Trace these right hand notes.

4. Draw 5 right hand quarter notes in the box below.

5. Draw 5 right hand half notes in the box below.

6. Trace these left hand notes

7. Draw 5 left hand quarter notes in the box below.

8. Draw 5 left hand half notes in the box below.

NOTES MOVE IN THREE WAYS:

Repeat

Up

Down

9. In the blanks below, label how each group of notes moves: Repeat, Up or Down

MUSICAL MASTERY

Ear Training

1. You will hear **LOW** notes and **HIGH** notes. Circle LOW if the note sounds low. Circle HIGH if the note sounds high.

1. LOW　　**HIGH**　　　　**2. LOW**　　**HIGH**　　　　**3. LOW**　　　**HIGH**

4. LOW　　**HIGH**　　　　**5. LOW**　　**HIGH**　　　　**6. LOW**　　　**HIGH**

2. You will hear groups of 3 notes. The notes will move UP or DOWN. Circle the pattern you hear.

1.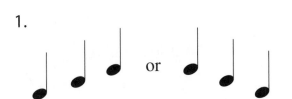

2.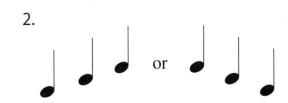

3.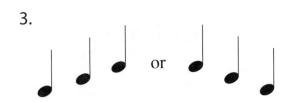

4.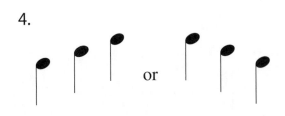

5.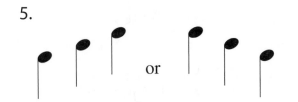

6.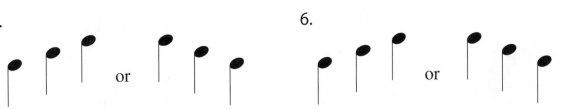

Symbol Mastery

1. Draw a line connecting each musical symbol to its name.

Symbol	Name
	Quarter Note
	Group of 2 Black Keys
	Whole Rest
	Half Note
	Double Bar Line
A B C D E F G	Quarter Rest
	Group of 3 Black Keys
	Music Alphabet
	Whole Note
	Repeat Sign
	Half Rest

Rhythm Mastery

1. Tap and count the rhythm pattern below. Remember:

   Stems Up = Right Hand   Stems Down = Left Hand

2. Now tap and count the rhythm pattern while your teacher plays an
   accompaniment.

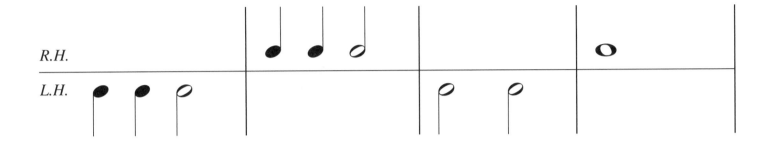

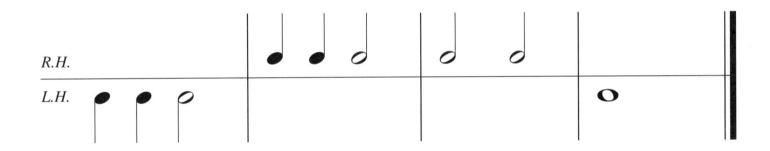

Accompaniment

The Staff

Music is written on a **STAFF**. The staff has 5 lines and 4 spaces.

5 Lines

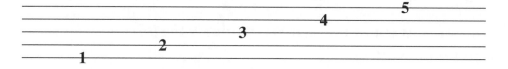

4 Spaces

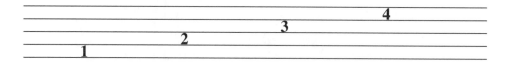

1. Number the lines.

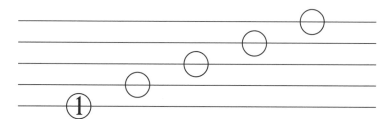

2. Number the spaces.

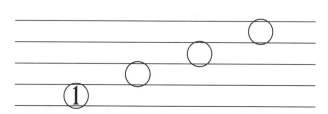

Notes are written on lines or in spaces of the staff.

Line Note   Space Note

3. Write L under the line notes and S under the space notes.

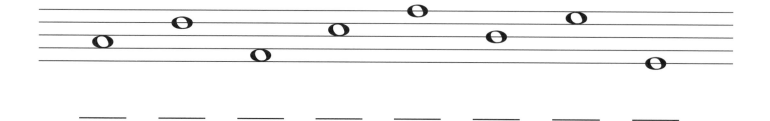

4. Draw whole notes on these lines.

5. Draw whole notes in these spaces.

line 3   line 5   line 2   line 4   line 1

space 1   space 3   space 2   space 4

STEPS on the staff move from a *space to the next line,*
or from a *line to the next space.*

6. Circle the answer that shows the direction of these notes.

Step Up	Step Up	Step Up	Step Up
Step Down	Step Down	Step Down	Step Down
Repeat	Repeat	Repeat	Repeat

7. Follow the directions and draw two more whole notes in each measure.
    The first one is done for you.

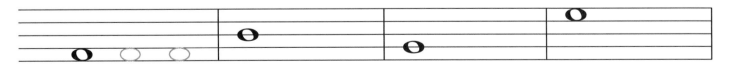

Repeat   Step Down   Step Up   Step Down

Treble Clef, Bass Clef and Grand Staff

 This is a **TREBLE CLEF**. Higher notes are written in the treble clef. The right hand usually plays notes in the treble clef.

 This is a **BASS CLEF**. Lower notes are written in the bass clef. The left hand usually plays notes in the bass clef.

1. Follow the steps to make a treble clef.

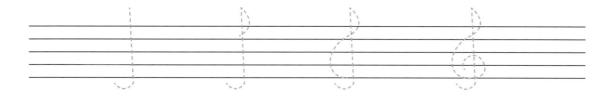

2. Now draw four of your own treble clefs.

3. Follow the steps to make a bass clef.

4. Now draw four of your own bass clefs.

This is a **GRAND STAFF**. It is formed by joining the treble staff and bass staff with a bar line and a brace.

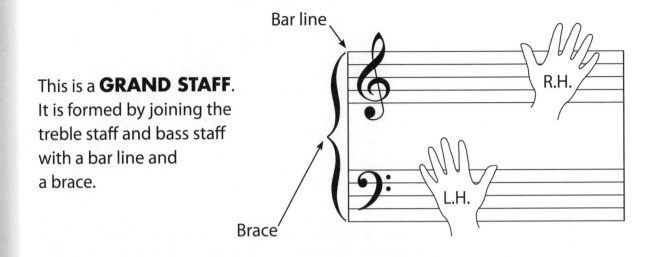

Below are 3 important **GUIDE NOTES** that will help you read music on the staff.

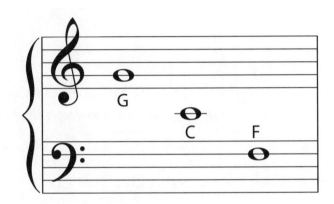

TREBLE G is on line 2 of the treble staff.

BASS F is on line 4 of the bass staff.

MIDDLE C is in the middle of the grand staff.

On your keyboard, place both thumbs on Middle C. You can play Treble G with your R.H. 5th finger and Bass F with your L.H. 5th finger.

5. Draw 5 more whole note G's on the G Line in the treble clef.

6. Draw 5 more whole note F's on the F Line in the bass clef.

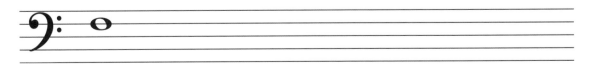

7. Draw 5 more whole note Middle C's on the treble staff.

8. Draw 5 more whole note Middle C's on the bass staff.

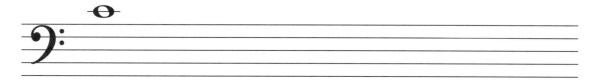

Since Middle C's are located between the Treble Staff and Bass Staff, they are written on short lines called **LEDGER LINES**.

9. Name each note below, either G or C.

10. Name each note below, either F or C.

Time Signatures, Rhythm and Dynamics

A **TIME SIGNATURE** at the beginning of the piece tells two things:

Top number = How many beats (or counts) are in each measure

Bottom number = What kind of note gets one beat (or count)

4 = 4 beats in a measure

4 = quarter note (♩) gets one beat

1. Draw bar lines after every 4 beats in the rhythms below. Add a double bar line at the end of each example.

2. Clap and count the rhythms.

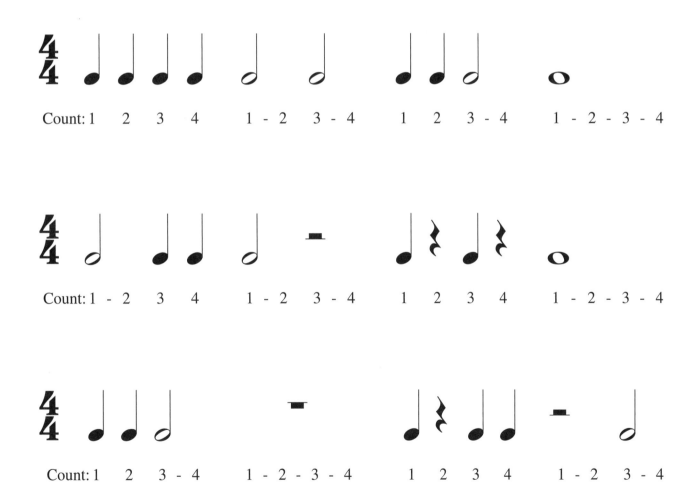

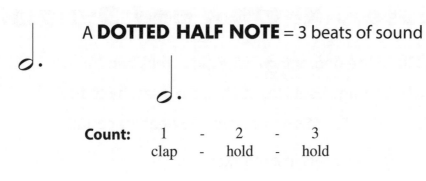

A **DOTTED HALF NOTE** = 3 beats of sound

Count: 1   -   2   -   3
clap - hold - hold

3 = 3 beats in a measure
4 = quarter note (♩) gets one beat

3. Draw bar lines after every 3 beats in the rhythm below.
   Add a double bar line at the end.

4. Clap and count the rhythm.

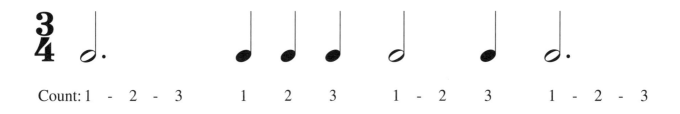

Count: 1 - 2 - 3   1   2   3   1 - 2   3   1 - 2 - 3

2 = 2 beats in a measure
4 = quarter note (♩) gets one beat

5. Draw bar lines after every 2 beats in the rhythm below.
   Add a double bar line at the end.

6. Clap and count the rhythm.

Count: 1 - 2   1   2   1   2   1 - 2

A **WHOLE REST** means to rest for a whole measure *in any time signature*.

7. Add the correct time signature in the boxes for the rhythms below.

8. Write the counts below each measure.

DYNAMIC SIGNS tell how soft or loud to play the music.

Italian Name	Sign (Symbol)	Meaning
piano	p	soft
forte	f	loud

9. Draw four more *piano* signs.

10. Draw four more *forte* signs.

MUSICAL MASTERY

Ear Training

1. You will hear 4 groups of rhythms. Circle the correct pattern.

1.

2.
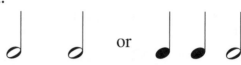

3.

4.

2. You will hear 4 groups of melodies. Circle the pattern that matches what you hear.

1.

2.

3.

4.

Symbol Mastery

1. Match the music symbol to its name by writing the correct number in the blank.

Symbol

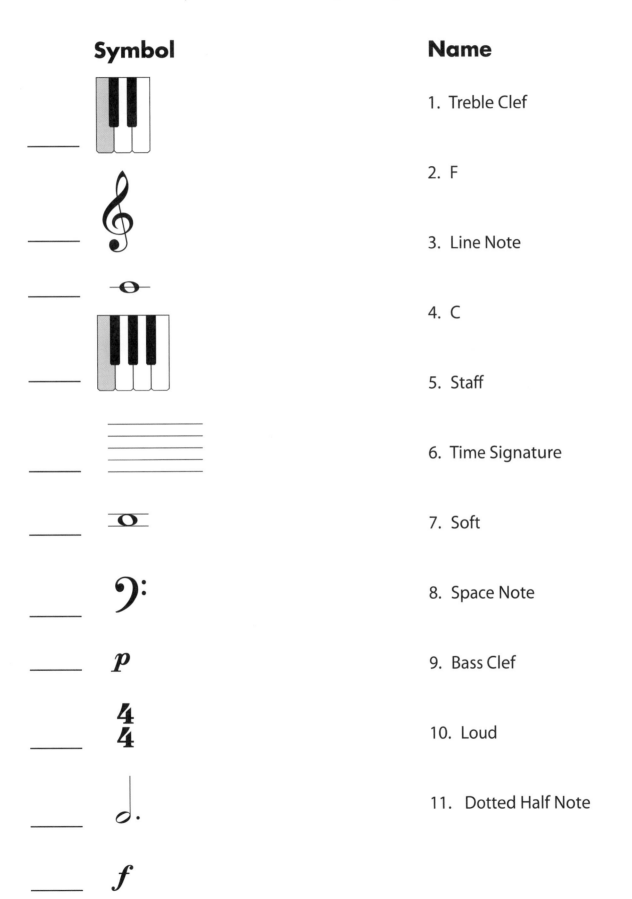

Name

1. Treble Clef

2. F

3. Line Note

4. C

5. Staff

6. Time Signature

7. Soft

8. Space Note

9. Bass Clef

10. Loud

11. Dotted Half Note

Reading Mastery

Using the guide notes you have learned, play "Evening Bells."

Evening Bells

Strong and steady

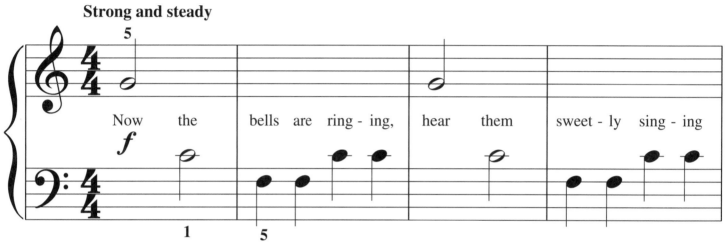

Hold down the right pedal (damper pedal) throughout.

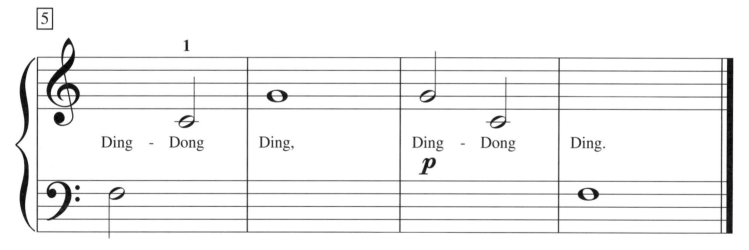

Accompaniment (Play both hands one octave higher throughout.)

Strong and steady (♩ = 120)

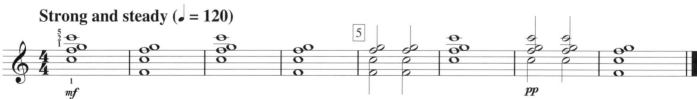

Steps and Skips

SKIPS on the keyboard skip one key and one letter name.

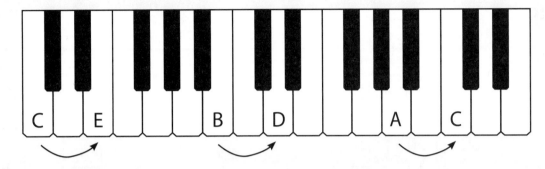

SKIPS on the staff move from *line to line* or *space to space*.

1. Circle either **STEP** or **SKIP** for each example.

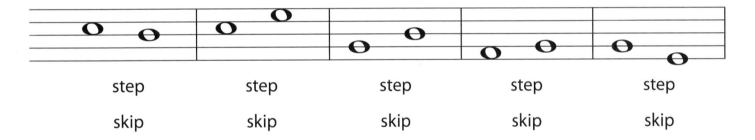

step	step	step	step	step
skip	skip	skip	skip	skip

2. Draw steps or skips from the given notes.

step down   skip up   step up   skip down   step down   skip up

TREBLE C is located *3 spaces up* from the middle of the grand staff.

BASS C is located *3 spaces down* from the middle of the grand staff.

MIDDLE C is located *in the middle* of the grand staff.

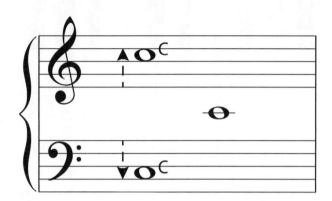

3. Draw 2 more Treble C's, 2 more Bass C's and 2 more Middle C's on the grand staff below.

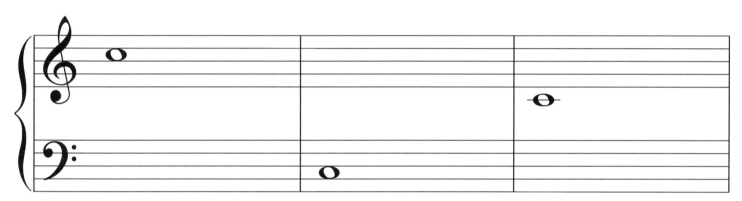

4. Label each note below: Treble C, Middle C or Bass C.

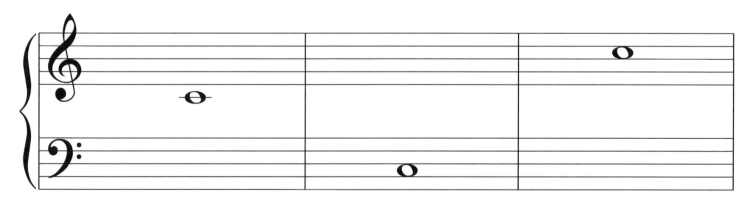

_____   _____   _____

Play Treble C, Bass C and Middle C on the keyboard.

Now you know **5 GUIDE NOTES** that will help you find other notes on the staff.

The Guide notes are: Bass C, Bass F, Middle C, Treble G and Treble C

5. Fill in each blank with the letter name of the note shown.

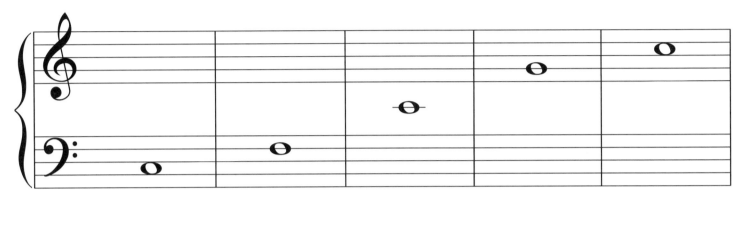

_____   _____   _____   _____   _____

6. Fill in the missing letters using the Music Alphabet.

C __ __ F __ __ __ C __ __ __ __ G __ __ C

7. On the grand staff below, notes are stepping up the staff. Fill in the blanks for the new notes using the Music Alphabet.

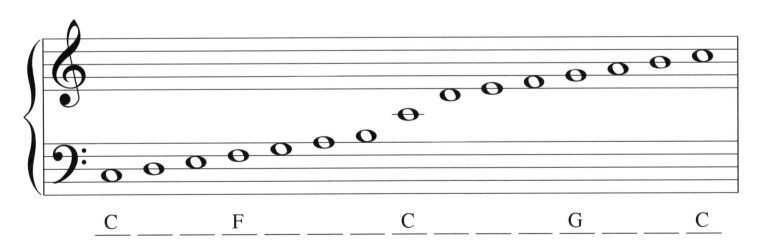

C __ __ F __ __ __ C __ __ __ __ G __ __ C

Stem Rule, 5-Finger Patterns and Review

Stem Rule

Stems go UP for notes below the middle line.
Up stems attach to the *right* side of the note head.

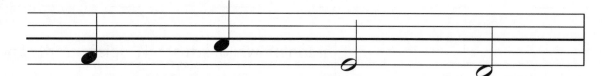

Stems go DOWN for notes on or above the middle line.
Down stems attach to the *left* side of the note head.

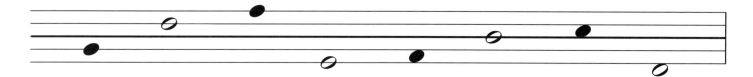

1. Add stems to the following notes. Follow the Stem Rule.

2. Name the following Guide Notes. Turn the whole notes into half notes by adding a stem to each note head.

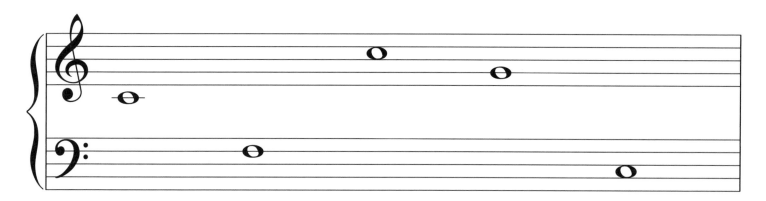

3. Write the Music Alphabet going forward.

A _____ _____ _____ _____ _____ _____

4. Write the Music Alphabet going backward.

_____ _____ _____ _____ _____ **G** _____

Practice saying the Music Alphabet forward and backward.
Mastering this skill will make reading music easier.

5. Name the following notes. Each set steps up or down from Guide Notes you have learned.

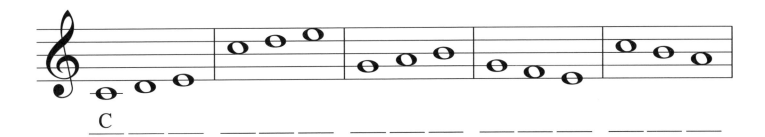

C _____ _____ _____ _____ _____ _____ _____ _____ _____ _____ _____ _____ _____ _____

F _____ _____ _____ _____ _____ _____ _____ _____ _____ _____ _____ _____ _____ _____

6. Turn the whole notes into half notes. Add a stem to each note head above.

7. Play each set of notes above.

To create a **5-FINGER PATTERN**, begin with the given note and name the next 4 notes stepping up. The lowest note names the pattern.

8. Write letter names to form 5-finger patterns on the keyboards below.

C Major

G Major

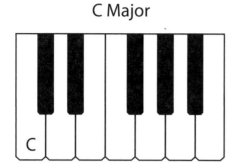
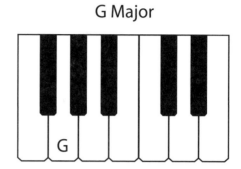

9. Draw the 5-finger patterns on the staff using whole notes. Notice the clef signs.

10. Add the missing Bar Lines to each staff below. Notice the time signature.

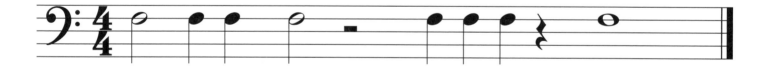

11. Write the correct counts under each measure above.

Remember: $\frac{4}{4}$ = 1 2 3 4 $\frac{3}{4}$ = 1 2 3

MUSICAL MASTERY

Ear Training

1. You will hear four sets of two notes. If the two notes sound the same, circle SAME. If the two notes sound different, circle DIFFERENT.

1.	2.	3.	4.
same	same	same	same
different	different	different	different

2. You will hear four different notes. Circle LOW if the note sounds low. Circle HIGH if the note sounds high.

1.	2.	3.	4.
high	high	high	high
low	low	low	low

3. You will hear four groups of notes. The notes will move up or down. Circle UP if the notes move up. Circle DOWN if the notes move down.

1.	2.	3.	4.
up	up	up	up
down	down	down	down

Musical Puzzle

Complete this crossword puzzle by writing the correct note names in the blanks.
Then fill in the puzzle squares with the correct musical term.

Across

3. m u s i __   __ l p h __ __ __ t

4. m __ __ s u r __

7. r __ p __ __ t

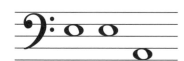

8. s p __ __ __

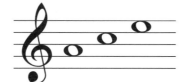

10. __ o r t __

Down

1. q u __ r t __ r   n o t __

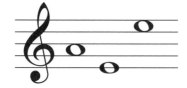

2. l i n __

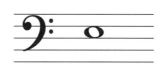

5. __ __ r   l i n __

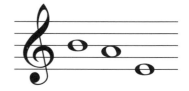

6. t r __ __ l __   __ l __ __

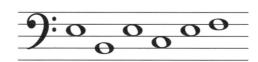

9. h __ l __   n o t __

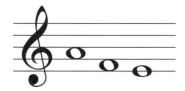

11. __ r __ n __   s t __ __ __

Musical Crossword Puzzle

Analysis

Study this folk tune, then answer the questions about it.

Yankee Doodle

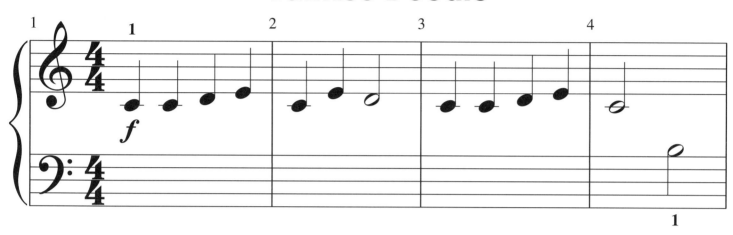

1. How many beats are in each measure?_____

2. What kind of note gets one beat? _____

3. How many half notes are in the piece? _____

4. Which measures have skips in them? _____ and _____

5. What does the "*f*" mean in measure 1? _____

6. Which measures have the exact same notes and rhythms? _____,

   _____ and _____.

BONUS: Play "Yankee Doodle" and demonstrate your musical mastery!

THEORY MASTERY

Review Test

1. Complete the music alphabet by filling in the blanks.

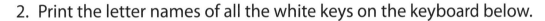

2. Print the letter names of all the white keys on the keyboard below.

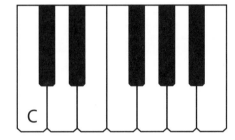

3. Fill in the blanks with the correct number.

   The music staff has _____ lines and _____ spaces.

4. Name the following guide notes on the treble staff and bass staff by filling in the blanks.

5. Write the music alphabet 2 times going up the keyboard. The first letter is printed for you.

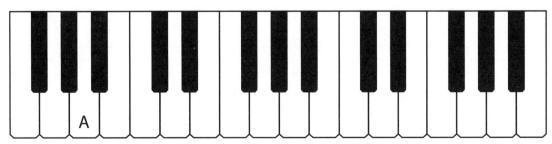

6. Circle the clef sign. Name the following notes.

____ ____ ____ ____ ____ ____

7. Circle the clef sign. Name the following notes.

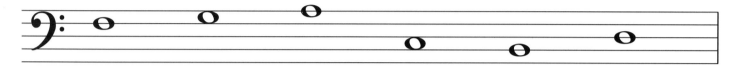

____ ____ ____ ____ ____ ____

8. Circle the music symbol that matches the name given.

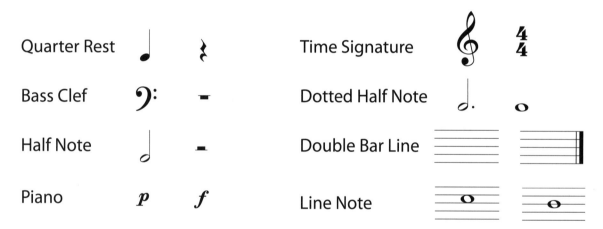

9. Draw whole notes on the staff for each letter given. Notice the clef sign.

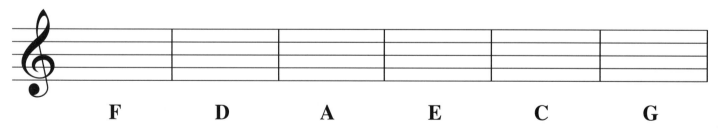

F   D   A   E   C   G

10. Draw whole notes on the staff for each letter given. Notice the clef sign.

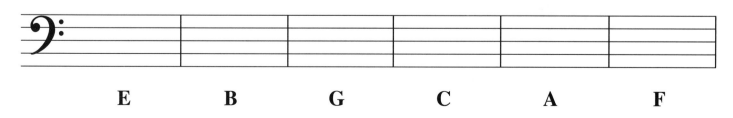

E   B   G   C   A   F

11. Draw the type of note named in each measure. Choose any line or space you wish, but remember the stem rule.

Quarter Note	Half Note	Dotted Half Note	Whole Note

12. The following pairs of notes move by step or skip. Circle the correct answer.

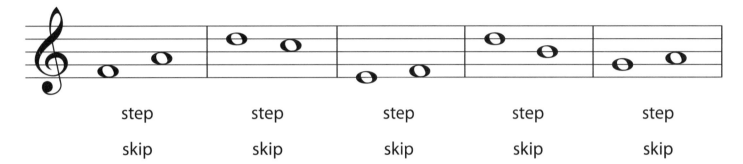

step	step	step	step	step
skip	skip	skip	skip	skip

13. Write the number of beats each note or rest receives in $\frac{4}{4}$ time.

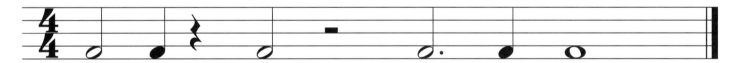

14. Add the missing bar lines on the staff below.

15. Write the counts below each note or rest.

Ear Training

1. You will hear low notes and high notes played one at a time. Circle the word that matches what you hear.

1.	2.	3.	4.	5.
high	high	high	high	high
low	low	low	low	low

2. You will hear groups of notes moving up or down. Circle the word that matches what you hear.

1.	2.	3.	4.	5.
up	up	up	up	up
down	down	down	down	down

3. Circle the music example you hear.

4. Circle the rhythm you hear.